Employee's Guide to Discrimination and Termination

Employee's Guide to Discrimination and Termination

Joanne Dekker, Esq.

Helpful Guides for Everyday Legal Matters

Parker Press Inc.

Contents

Contents

What This Book's About

Many aspects of an employment relationship protect you in the workplace. This book explains how discrimination laws work in the workplace—and what your rights are if you're terminated.

At the beginning of every employment relationship, both employees and employers have expectations about how their relationship will work. But if things go wrong, expectations are not met and the relationship sours, what are your rights as an employee?

There are federal and state laws in place that not only protect you as an employee, but that also give you certain rights and avenues of redress if your employer oversteps its bounds. These laws include:

- Wage and hour laws.

- Laws prohibiting illegal discrimination in the workplace.

- Workplace safety laws.

- Workers' Compensation laws for employees injured on the job.

- Benefits, both before and after you leave your employment.

- Laws protecting "whistle blowers."

In this book we focus on issues that arise when you experience forms of illegal discrimination, consider suing your employer, or your employment is terminated. We'll let you know when we think it makes sense for you to hire a lawyer to help protect your rights. Other Real Life Legal™ publications will cover subjects not discussed in this book.

If an employer is looking for ways to fire employees, or you find yourself being harassed by a superior or your co-workers, then understanding how the law works can help you navigate the stormy seas of a troubled workplace environment.

Workplace Rights

The general flow of U.S. workplace laws is to protect workers from unsafe conditions and workplace policies that discriminate, but there is a lot of fine print. These laws change as society seeks to address growing problems or concerns.

A century ago, workplace laws focused on making work places safer, protecting against child labor and later providing minimum wages. About forty years ago, laws were passed to protect pensions. Now they cover different things.

- The first law to protect against worker discrimination was the Equal Pay Act of 1963 that made it illegal to pay men and women at different rates for the same work.

- Congress passed Title VII of the Civil Rights Act of 1964 that made it illegal to discriminate on the bases of race, color, religion, national origin or sex. Title VII also prohibits employers from retaliating against anyone who reports illegal discrimination or assists in an investigation or lawsuit involving illegal discrimination.

Non-discrimination laws aim to create equal treatment for all workers in the United States, regardless of heritage, age, gender or disability. When these rights are violated, workers have the right to take legal action against their employers.

Although the federal government passes and enforces the "sweeping" laws, states and localities also pass laws that may expand these federally-established rights. For example, the Age Discrimination in Employment Act (discussed on page 19) only applies to individuals age forty or older. Some states have passed laws prohibiting discrimination based on age for any employee over the age of eighteen.

Laws that apply to "employers" also typically apply to "other covered entities" such as labor unions and employment agencies. Federal employees are also protected by these laws (although some of the remedies may differ for federal employees).

If an area of workplace law is regulated by the federal government, states can enact more favorable protections for employees. For example, if federal law stipulates that "minimum" wage is $8/hour, a state can mandate minimum wage at $9/hour, but not $7/hour.

State and local laws can also regulate and protect industries or professions that are integral to local economies. For example, coastal states may enact laws to protect fishermen, or states with significant high tech industries such as Washington and California may enact laws to protect employees and contractors who work in those industries.

Workers at Small Companies May Not Be Protected

You have to read the fine print to see if federal laws designed to protect you bind your employer:

- Most federal laws that prohibit discrimination in the workplace only apply to employers with fifteen or more employees.

- The Equal Pay Act applies to employers with one employee.

- The Age Discrimination in Employment Act applies to employers with twenty or more employees.

- State laws may have their own rules regarding what employers are covered.

Certain types of discrimination are not protected by federal laws.

Illegal Discrimination

Illegal discrimination occurs when an employer does not follow the law and discriminates against a person in a "protected class."

3

Every employee is entitled to a workplace free from illegal discrimination, harassment and retaliation, and employers may not illegally discriminate against employees or job applicants at any time during the employment process. What this means is that "discrimination" cannot occur:

- During the hiring process.

- At any time while the employee is employed.

- As employment is being terminated.

Illegal Employment Discrimination Explained

Discrimination is clear if an employer deliberately refuses to hire people of a particular religion or ethnic background. An employer cannot discriminate on this basis and those discriminated against are in a "protected class." But discrimination is not always so clear. To give rise to a claim of discrimination, the employer's action must be prohibited.

Not all types of "unequal" treatment are necessarily "illegal."

For example, Employer A may decide that it likes to hire married people because they have proven to be more loyal. Employer B may choose to hire a slim, fit sales force because it gives a better image in its retail shops. These practices may not be illegal discrimination in and of themselves, if "unmarried people" or overweight people are not a "protected class." However, if Employer B refuses to hire people age forty and older that are in good shape, then it may be violating the Age Discrimination in Employment Act.

REAL LIFE EXAMPLE

Mary interviews for a job with TechCo. The interviewer is about to make her a job offer when Mary mentions that she is a single parent with young children. The interviewer is concerned that Mary may miss too much work time if her children get sick, and he decides not to hire her.

Mary's status as a mother of young children may not put her in a "protected" class for purposes of employment discrimination. However, if TechCo hires a similarly qualified male candidate who is a single parent with young children, then Mary may have a claim on the basis of gender discrimination because the job was given to a male in the same circumstances and not to a female.

Federal Laws Prohibiting Discrimination

There are many federal laws that prohibit discrimination for many reasons. Not all forms of discrimination are prohibited.

Federal law makes it illegal to discriminate on the basis of:

- Age
- Disability
- Equal Pay/Compensation
- Genetic Information
- Harassment
- National Origin
- Pregnancy
- Race/Color
- Religion
- Retaliation
- Gender

Discrimination Based on Race, Color, National Origin, Religion and Gender

"Title VII of the Civil Rights Act of 1964 (Title VII)" prohibits discrimination on the basis of race, color, religion, national origin and sex, including gender bias and sexual harassment. Title VII also makes it illegal to retaliate against anyone who reports illegal discrimination or participates in any investigation or legal proceedings relating to employment discrimination.

Title VII requires employers to make a reasonable accommodation for persons with "sincerely held religious beliefs," unless the accommodation would make it unreasonably difficult for the employer to do business in an effective way.

Discrimination Based on Age

The **"Age Discrimination in Employment Act (ADEA)"** protects workers who are age forty and older. The ADEA does not protect workers under age forty, although some states have laws that protect younger workers. It should be noted that illegal discrimination under the ADEA can also occur even if *both* workers are over the age of forty.

REAL LIFE EXAMPLE

Diamond's Department Store hires fifty-five-year-old Wanda and twenty-five-year-old Tracy to sell men's cologne. Diamond's discovers that when Tracy is working, the counter is packed with young men who buy cologne. Sales are not as robust when Wanda is on the sales floor. Diamond's decides that young and pretty women sell more cologne than older women. Diamond's hires another young female salesperson and fires Wanda. Wanda may have a cause of action under the ADEA if she was let go because of her age.

Waivers Under the ADEA

When employees leave a job, employers often ask for a signed release and waiver of any claims that the employee could "potentially" have because of the employment relationship. Employers do this to protect themselves against a lawsuit.

A waiver or release under the ADEA must meet very specific criteria. A waiver or release that fails to meet these specific criteria may be considered invalid, which means that you retain your right to sue your employer for ADEA violations.

To be enforceable, your ADEA waiver must be "knowing and voluntary." To be "knowing and voluntary" the waiver must:

- Be in writing and *written in "plain language,"* taking into account an employee's level of education and understanding.

- Not mislead, exaggerate or minimize the benefits or limitations of the terms and conditions of the agreement.

- Include a provision that the employee is not releasing any future rights or claims you may have after the date the waiver is executed.

By law, an ADEA waiver must:

- Advise you *in writing to consult with an attorney* prior to executing the agreement;

- *Give you something in addition to whatever else you are already entitled to upon termination of employment.* For example, if you are already entitled to receive payment for unused vacation time, the payment to you for unused vacation is *not enough* to make the agreement valid. The employer must give you something more, such as severance pay.

ADEA WAIVERS: Watch for Mandatory Time Restrictions

- The waiver agreement must give you at least *twenty-one days* to consider the agreement. This time period is extended to forty-five days when the ADEA waiver is offered with an exit incentive to a group or class of employees.

- The waiver agreement must inform *you that you have seven days after signing the agreement to revoke the waiver.* You should be aware that the agreement does not become effective or enforceable by either you or your employer until after the seven days have passed. This seven-day period *cannot* be shortened—not even by agreement of the parties.

If a benefit was eliminated in violation of law or contract, an offer to reinstate the benefit in exchange for a waiver is not valid for the purposes of the ADEA.

If you ever find yourself being asked to sign an ADEA waiver, it's a good idea to consult with a lawyer to make sure your rights are protected. Often these are offered as part of a separation or termination agreement and a lot can be at stake.

Discrimination Based on Pregnancy

The **"Pregnancy Discrimination Act (PDA)"** prohibits any form of employment discrimination based on pregnancy. The PDA requires:

- That an employer treat a woman who is temporarily unable to perform her job due to complications arising from her pregnancy as if she were a temporarily disabled employee.

- That an employer offer alternate assignments to pregnant women if they offer temporarily disabled employees light duty or alternative assignments.

In some instances, temporary impairments brought on by pregnancy such as gestational diabetes may be covered by the Americans with Disabilities Act, even though pregnancy itself is not a disability under the ADA.

REAL LIFE EXAMPLES

Tracy has been working at Diamond's and is the top seller of men's cologne. When she tells her manager that she is pregnant, Diamond's fires Tracy because they don't believe that men will want to buy cologne from a pregnant woman. Diamond's has violated the PDA.

If Tracy is not fired but begins to have some complications with her pregnancy and her doctor tells her that she may not stand on her feet all day, then Diamond's may make an adjustment. For example, if Diamond's has a "light-duty" policy, then it must offer Tracy an alternative assignment or accommodation, such as letting her perform office work at a desk or providing her with a chair while working at the counter.

Discrimination Based on Genetic Information

Title II of the **"Genetic Information Nondiscrimination Act of 2008 (GINA)"** prohibits an employer from using or obtaining genetic information about a person or the person's family in order to make employment decisions. GINA covers information about an employee's genetic tests or the genetic tests of the employee's family member. It also includes general family medical history.

GINA's protections are aimed at preventing employers from assessing whether an employee or applicant has a propensity to be affected by a medical condition, such as cancer or a mood disorder.

An employer may obtain some genetic or health information to comply with certification requirements under the **"Family and Medical Leave Act (FMLA)"** to monitor the effect of toxic substances in the workplace, or if the employer is a forensic laboratory and conducts testing for DNA analysis for law enforcement agencies.

Equal Pay for Equal Work

The **"Equal Pay Act (EPA)"** requires employers to pay men and women at the same rate for the same work. The jobs do not have to be identical, but the job duties must be substantially equal. The EPA covers wages and benefits such as vacation time, health insurance and profit sharing.

Discrimination Based on Disabilities

Sweeping legislation known as the Americans with Disabilities Act (ADA) prevents discrimination at work and elsewhere for disabled individuals.

"The Americans with Disabilities Act (ADA)" prohibits discrimination in the workplace because a person has a disability. The Rehabilitation Act (commonly known as the "Rehab Act"), provides federal employees with essentially the same protections as the ADA.

In addition to protecting individuals who have a disability, the ADA also protects:

- Persons who may have a history of having a disability.

- Persons who are perceived as having a disability.

- Workers who have a relationship with a person with a disability, e.g., a father who has an autistic child or a person whose parent has bipolar disorder.

The ADA is especially overrun with "legalese" and "lawyer speak" which make it hard for laymen to understand. For example, the ADA says that you cannot discriminate against: "a qualified individual with a disability who can perform the *essential job functions* with or without a *reasonable accommodation* unless in doing so it causes the employer an *undue hardship.*" What does all that really mean? Stick with us, and we'll get you through this maze.

REAL LIFE EXAMPLE

Keisha has epilepsy and suffers from mild-to-severe seizures. Her certified service dog, Malcolm, is able to detect when she is about to have a seizure and alerts her so that she can find a place to lie down until her seizure is over. Keisha applies for a job in the catering sales department at Ace Hotel. The job requires each catering sales employee to share an office with one other coworker and to show clients and potential clients around the hotel's facilities, including dining rooms and the kitchen.

Keisha tells the Catering Director that she needs reasonable accommodations that include bringing Malcolm to work and taking him out for potty breaks at least twice a day. She also requests that she be provided with a private room where she can lie down in the event that Malcolm detects the onset of a seizure.

The Catering Director is excited at the prospect of hiring Keisha as she has a proven track record at her previous job. However, the Catering Director is concerned that Health Department regulations do not allow animals in the kitchen or other areas where food is being prepared or stored and that Keisha will not be able to perform this part of her job.

Under the ADA, Keisha's epilepsy is a "disability" because it interferes with and/or restricts at least one major life activity, e.g., the ability to control her body. Keisha has asked for "reasonable accommodations" that would not be an "undue hardship" on her employer, e.g., bringing Malcolm to work and taking him for potty breaks, and finding a designated private room for her in the event Malcolm alerts her, or giving her a private office.

Ace Hotel can also offer Keisha a reasonable accommodation with respect to the "essential job function" of showing customers the kitchen and related areas. For example, another catering sales employee could be asked to show the customer these areas while Keisha and Malcolm wait outside. Ace Hotel could also allow Keisha to have her own office rather than share one with a coworker, allowing her the privacy she needs if she has a seizure.

This is just one example of how the ADA is interpreted and applied.

Common Questions: Legal Terms and the ADA

- What is a disability?
- What is an "undue hardship?"
- What is an "essential job function?"
- What type of "reasonable accommodation" must an employer provide?
- Who decides what is "reasonable?"

What Is a "Disability" Under the ADA?

For purposes of the ADA, you have a disability if:

1. *You have a physical or mental impairment that substantially limits one or more major life activities.* A major life activity includes walking, standing, talking, caring for oneself, seeing and hearing. "Major life activities" also include the function of individual organs and systems within the body, such as the digestive system, kidneys, circulatory system and lungs.

2. *You have a history of a physical or mental impairment that substantially limited a major life activity in the past but you may not have it now.* A person whose cancer is in remission would be an example.

3. *The disability you have is not temporary in nature—e.g., it is not going to go away in six months.* If you have lifting restrictions while you recover from surgery, then that is temporary and you are not protected by the ADA. However, if you have lifting restrictions because you have arthritis in your back, then you would be protected by the ADA.

Short- vs. Long-Term Disability

The ADA recognizes that both permanent disabilities and short-term or intermittent disabilities can *substantially limit* a major life activity. For example, a permanent and total disability would be the loss of the use of your legs. A person with epilepsy may only suffer from seizures once or twice a year. In the example with Keisha, above, she doesn't know when she will have a seizure or how bad it might be. She is still protected by the ADA.

Disabled People Must Still Be Able to Perform the "Essential Job Functions"

To be protected against discrimination under the ADA (i.e., a "qualified individual with a disability"), an applicant or employee must still be able to do the job.

The ADA requires that a disabled person demonstrate that he or she is qualified to perform the essential job duties through education, training, skills and/or experience. If you cannot perform the "essential job functions," then you are not qualified for the job, and the issue of disability doesn't matter.

The ADA and the **"Code of Federal Regulations (CFR)"** have established two sets of the guidelines concerning "essential job functions." A job function is considered to be an essential job function if any one of the following is true:

- The job exists to perform that function. For example, the essential job function of a chef is to cook.

- Only a few employees can perform the job.

- The function is so highly specialized that the employer only hires people for the job because of their expertise in performing that function. For example, surgeons are hired by a medical practice because of their expertise in performing surgery.

REAL LIFE EXAMPLE

Dawn is an account executive at TechCo. Her job is to contact clients, make sales and develop marketing strategies. She is also required to go to the warehouse at least twice a week to check on orders, and she sometimes assists with inventory.

Dawn's allergies have worsened over the years and she suffers from severe asthma attacks when subjected to certain allergens and other air-quality deficiencies. Sometimes when she goes to the warehouse she has asthma attacks, and may be ill for several days after.

Dawn's work at the warehouse will probably not be considered to be one of her essential job functions.

Even if it was, there are other employees who can check on her orders and other people can perform inventory. A reasonable accommodation would be for Dawn to be excused from going to the warehouse.

Factors to Consider to Determine Essential Job Functions

- What does the job description say?
- Does the position exist to perform the function?
- How much time does the employee spend on the function?
- What happens if the function is not performed?
- Are other employees available to perform the function?
- Is there any expertise or skill required to perform the function?
- In some instances, a collective bargaining agreement between the employer and a union may establish what the essential job functions are for the represented employees.

You Are Disabled But Can Do the Job. Now What?

If you can perform the "essential job functions," the law next looks at what the employer can be required to do so you can do the job. This is known as a "reasonable accommodation." Employers are not required to take extraordinary measures to enable a qualified individual to work.

How Do You Decide If an Accommodation Is "Reasonable"?

A **"reasonable accommodation"** is a change to a qualified individual's working conditions to allow that person to perform the essential functions of the job. If a qualified individual requests a reasonable accommodation, the employer and the employee or applicant must work together to achieve a reasonable accommodation.

- An employee or job applicant can suggest a specific reasonable accommodation based on the essential job functions and the employee's knowledge of his limitations in performing the work.

- The employer is not required to give the employee the exact reasonable accommodation requested. It may provide an alternative accommodation as long as it allows the employee to perform the essential functions of the job.

An employer may not have to provide a reasonable accommodation if providing a reasonable accommodation would cause the employer an undue hardship.

What Causes Employers "Undue Hardship?"

Factors to consider when determining if the employer would experience an undue hardship include:

- The cost of the accommodation.

- The employer's financial capability to provide the accommodation.

- The size and nature of the business.

REAL LIFE EXAMPLE

Cargo Pants International interviews Bob for a position operating fabric and pattern cutting machinery. Bob has excellent job qualifications and there is no doubt he can perform the essential job functions. However, Bob is wheelchair bound and when he reports to work on his first day he realizes that many of the machines are geared for employees to sit on "bar stool" height chairs to do their jobs making it impossible for Bob to perform the work. Bob requests a reasonable accommodation and suggests that the company buy a $40,000 machine that is at the height that allows him to do the job from his wheelchair.

Cargo Pants discovers that it can purchase and install levers on the existing machinery that will lower the tables to a height where Bob is comfortable working. The cost to buy and install the levers is $1,000. Cargo Pants makes the modifications to the machines so that Bob can work. Cargo Pants has met its obligation to provide Bob with a reasonable accommodation that allows Bob to perform the essential job functions.

Employers Can't Ask About Disabilities

With very limited exceptions, it is a violation of the ADA for an employer to ask an applicant or an existing employee if he has a disability. But the employer can ask if the individual can perform all the duties of the job, or how the individual would perform the job, with or without a reasonable accommodation.

In some instances, a disability will be obvious, such as blindness or Bob's wheelchair (above). Other disabilities are not so obvious, such as diabetes, asthma or arthritis. And some disabilities develop or worsen over time, or are the result of an accident or illness.

Employers may not require a medical examination of an applicant during the application process or interview stage.

Once the employer makes a job offer, it may make the job conditional on the applicant passing a medical examination or answering medical questions, *but only if* all applicants for the same type of job are required to do the same.

Your employer may not ask medical questions about your disability or health unless the employer needs medical documentation to support your request for a reasonable accommodation. The employer may also ask you for information if the employer believes that you cannot perform a job successfully or safely because of a medical condition.

Discrimination Based on Sexual Orientation

There is no federal law that prohibits discrimination against gays, lesbians, bisexual or transgender individuals. Many state and local government have enacted laws that make this discrimination illegal.

While many people believe that discrimination based on someone's status as gay, lesbian or transgender is illegal, in fact there is presently no national law that bans discrimination for these reasons. Instead, states and local municipalities have passed laws that make it illegal to discriminate against people based on their sexual orientation and gender identity. But even these laws are uneven on who's protected and which employers are subject to them.

Contrary to popular belief, there is no nationwide law that protects against discrimination based on sexual orientation or gender status. In some places you can legally be fired for being gay or transgender.

Presently, twenty-one states and the District of Columbia make it illegal to fire or discriminate against someone because of their sexual orientation. Yet only eighteen of those states protect transgender employees. About 200 municipalities protect against this type of discrimination.

For example:

- California and Colorado ban sexual orientation and gender identity discrimination.

- New York and Wisconsin ban sexual orientation discrimination but not gender identity discrimination.

- Florida and Pennsylvania offer no protections.

Even if a state or local law is in place to protect against discrimination, read the fine print! In Illinois, Maryland, Nevada and New Mexico, these anti-discrimination laws do not bind employers with fewer than fifteen employees.

To learn more about which states have laws to prevent these types of discrimination, check out: https://www.aclu.org/maps/non-discrimination-laws-state-state-information-map

Which Discriminatory Actions Are Illegal?

In looking at which actions may give rise to a lawsuit, it is important to remember that not all harassment or discrimination is illegal.

Employers may treat their employees badly or discriminate against them for reasons that are not illegal. Bad management is not necessarily illegal, but sometimes it's hard to tell when your employer has discriminated against you.

Discrimination can take the following forms:

- **"Disparate Impact"**: An employment policy looks fair or neutral but is not;

- **"Disparate Treatment"**: Similarly situated employees are treated differently for reasons which are against the law;

- **"Hostile Workplace Environment"**: A work environment where harassment or discrimination is so severe or pervasive that a reasonable person would consider it abusive, hostile or intimidating;

- **"Sexual Harassment"**: A form of hostile work environment, but also extends to situations where sexual favors are demanded in exchange for a job benefit (including keeping your job or getting a promotion);

- **"Retaliation"**: This occurs when employment decisions are taken against you because you reported discrimination or participated in an investigation or proceeding relating to illegal discrimination.

Disparate (or Adverse) Impact

Disparate impact occurs when an employer's policy appears fair or neutral on its face, but in fact *has the effect of* discriminating against one or more protected classes of employees. Employment policies and job descriptions and requirements should reasonably relate to the actual job being performed and to the employer's business.

Employers sometimes claim that their policies are either a *business necessity* or establish a **"Bona Fide Occupational Qualification (BFOQ)"**. A BFOQ must be reasonably essential to the job requirements. The burden is generally on the employer to demonstrate that its policy is necessary. Here are a few examples:

- Ace Hotel requires its front desk staff, bell staff and housekeeping staff to wear uniforms. The dress code prohibits all employees from wearing hats or head coverings. On its face, this policy seems reasonable. However, many religions require their members to cover their heads. The hotel's policy *has the effect of* discriminating against these employees on the basis of their religion. Ace Hotel must allow these employees to wear head coverings.

- Big Manufacturing Company runs an assembly line that uses conveyor belts and other machinery with moving parts. As a safety precaution, Big prohibits assembly line employees from wearing scarves, loose clothing and jewelry. Big's policy would be acceptable, but it might have to allow some workers to wear a modified head covering.

- Diamond's Department Store presents fashion shows several times a year. Diamond's advertises for women to model women's clothing and men to model the men's clothing. This would be an example of a bona fide occupational qualification.

Disparate (or Adverse) Treatment

Disparate treatment occurs when your employer treats you differently than other similarly-situated employees *because of* your membership in a protected class. "Similarly-situated" generally means that you have the same job and same supervisor as your coworkers. It also occurs in the hiring process when applicants are denied employment *because of* their membership in a protected class.

REAL LIFE EXAMPLE

Mandy has worked for Ace Hotel as a front desk clerk for two years. She is a sophomore in college and is studying to become a teacher. She is paid $9.50 an hour and generally works fifteen to twenty-five hours per week. Her job duties include making reservations, greeting guests and checking them into their rooms.

Simon also works part-time for Ace as a front desk clerk and has the same duties as Mandy. He has worked for Ace for one year and earns $9.00. Simon has just graduated with a degree in accounting. Simon is offered and accepts an entry-level job in the hotel's accounting department and receives a raise to $15.00 an hour.

Ace Hotel hires Alex to take Simon's place as a front desk clerk. Alex has never worked at a hotel. His previous jobs include working at a coffee shop and in the shipping department at Diamond's Department Store. Ace Hotel pays Alex $11.50 an hour.

Mandy meets with the general manager and asks for a raise. She claims that she should receive a raise because Simon received one. She also claims that she should be paid more than Alex because he has no experience and she has been working for Ace for two years. The general manager tells Mandy that Alex is paid more because he is a man with a family to support.

Has Ace Hotel illegally discriminated against Mandy?
Yes and no.

With respect to new-hire Alex, Ace Hotel has illegally discriminated against Mandy on the basis of her gender. It cannot pay Alex more than Mandy just because he is male. Mandy and Alex are "similarly-situated" because they have the same job at the hotel.

What about Simon? Ace Hotel has acted legally with respect to Simon. Simon has been promoted to a different position in a different department because of his qualifications, including a degree in accounting. He and Mandy are no longer "similarly-situated."

Hostile Work Environment

As an employee, you are entitled to a workplace free from illegal harassment based on your race, color, religion, age, gender, genetic information, national origin, pregnancy or disability.

Harassment becomes illegal when being forced to deal with the harassing behavior becomes a condition of your employment, or the harassment becomes so severe or pervasive that a reasonable person would consider it abusive, hostile or intimidating.

Being forced to deal with annoying or petty behavior can be stressful but it's generally not considered illegal harassment. Isolated instances also usually don't create a hostile work environment unless the action is considered severe.

Illegal harassing behavior can include offensive jokes, pictures or objects, slurs or epithets, name calling, threats, intimidation, mockery, insults and interference with your work.

What You Need to Know About a Hostile Work Environment

- A hostile work environment can be created by your supervisor, another supervisor, your coworkers and even non-employees such as vendors or customers.

- You can be a victim of a hostile work environment even if you are not the intended target of the harassment. If you have to listen to your coworker being abused because of his race then you may also have an actionable claim.

- You don't have to lose your job to have a claim for a hostile work environment. If your mental or physical health declines because of the harassment then you may be able to recover damages.

Sexual Harassment

Sexual harassment is a form of illegal discrimination based on gender and/or a hostile work environment. It can be male against female, female against male or same sex harassment.

As with other forms of hostile work environment, offhand comments, teasing or isolated incidents will generally not constitute sexual harassment. Instead, the harassing behavior must become "severe and pervasive." The comments or actions must also be unwelcome.

Any demand for sexual favors in exchange for a job benefit is illegal. Job benefits include, but are not limited to, being hired, maintaining your job, getting a raise or being promoted.

Take Action If You Are Being Harassed!

Follow the protocol in your employee handbook, if there is one. If not:

- Tell the harasser you find the conduct offensive and that you want it to stop, whether you are the intended victim of the harassment or adversely affected by the hostile work environment.

- If you are not comfortable telling your harasser to stop, you should report the conduct to your manager or other supervisor.

- If that is not possible, report the complaint to the human resource department or other designated person or office (like Human Resources) that will address your issues.

Your failure to report harassment to company management may result in your not being able to successfully pursue a claim of discrimination in a lawsuit.

Retaliation

When your employer tries to get back at you for speaking up about your rights or taking action to uphold them, their "retaliation" is also a violation of the law.

Federal and state laws also protect you from retaliation for reporting illegal discrimination and/or for participating in any investigation or lawsuit relating to the illegal discrimination. Retaliation includes any *adverse employment action* such as termination, demotion, a pay cut, having assignments taken away or having your hours changed.

REAL LIFE EXAMPLE

Phil works at Big Box Appliances. He is Jewish and wears a yarmulke at work. In observance of the Sabbath, Phil leaves work before sundown on Friday and does not return until Sunday. Phil's new manager, Tom, starts making jokes about Phil's yarmulke and all the time he takes off on weekends to go fishing. Phil follows company policy and files a complaint with the HR office. HR investigates Phil's complaint and interviews Phil, Tom and Phil's coworker, Kira.

Kira confirms that Tom has made inappropriate comments to and about Phil because of Phil's religion. Tom is formally reprimanded and suspended for one week without pay. Upon his return, he reduces and changes Kira's hours so that she is less likely to make sales commissions. Tom reassigns Phil to the warehouse to take inventory, thus also preventing Phil from earning sales commissions.

Tom has illegally retaliated against Phil and Kira for engaging in protected activity. They should report Tom's retaliatory actions to management.

Illegal Terminations

If you are fired for an illegal reason, you may be able to bring a lawsuit against your employer.

9

What Is Wrongful Termination?

You may know you are being terminated because of a reduction in force or your position is being eliminated. But what if you can't quite put your finger on what the termination is about—but believe it may be because of your race, or you speak English with an accent or some other reason that just seems "not right?"

A **"wrongful termination"** occurs when an employee is fired for a reason that is considered "illegal." If your employer fires you because of illegal discrimination, then the firing is a violation of law and considered a wrongful termination.

If you are fired and happen to be in a protected class, that alone may not mean your firing is a wrongful termination.

REAL LIFE EXAMPLE

Barry works for AAA Accounting Software at the "help desk." Barry is a fifty-three-year-old CPA who had worked for accounting firms and was familiar with the software, but had never worked a help desk. After being out of work for a year, he was glad for the job.

All help desk employees at AAA Accounting Software are "graded" based on certain metrics including: number of calls taken, time spent on each call, difficulty of the subject matter covered in the call and feedback from customers. Internal systems can monitor the length of the call and recordings reveal the difficulty of the subject matter covered. AAA has intensive training and monitoring systems and likes to hire employees who are accountants who have used the program. It has a three-month training and trial period and then an additional review at six months, at which point it terminates underperforming new hires.

Barry's supervisor, Emile, is a thirty-seven-year-old Hispanic man who has a tech background. Most of Barry's colleagues are women under age forty and none of them is a CPA. Emile spends a lot of time flirting and bantering with the women who work the help desk phone bank.

After intensive training and two months working the help desk, Emile informs Barry that he is fielding half the number of calls as his colleagues and must speed it up. Emile reports that Barry: (1) spends too much time socializing with callers and/or (2) doesn't know the program as well as he should. Barry has also received poor ratings on customer feedback. Barry is terminated at six months and told his numbers did not meet the job requirements.

Barry wants to sue AAA claiming he was fired because he was not Emile's "type." Barry will need proof that his firing was on account of his gender and/or his age and not his poor performance. Barry is a member of the protected classes of age, gender, race and national origin. But that alone does not alone make Barry's firing a "wrongful termination."

What Is a Constructive Discharge?

When your life at work is made so miserable that you have no choice but to quit, there may be an issue as to whether there has been a "constructive discharge." This occurs when illegal working conditions are so bad, that you've essentially been forced out. This can occur in situations such as a hostile work environment.

Constructive discharge, like wrongful termination, is very dependent on the facts and what you can prove. When you consider suing your employer, you must have an idea of what you can prove—not just how you feel.

BE PREPARED FOR THE LONG HAUL

Even if you have a strong case against your employer for illegally terminating your employment, be prepared for a long and bumpy road.

- The EEOC and the courts have notoriously long backlogs of cases.

- Employers may attempt to delay proceedings.

- Employers may try to make you look like a "bad employee," and that it had valid reasons for terminating your employment.

An attorney who specializes in your issues will help guide you through the rough spots.

What Happens If I Think My Employer Has Violated My Rights?

It's not always easy to decide what to do if your rights are violated. But under the law, you have options. A first step may be to contact your state's Department of Labor or the federal Equal Employment Opportunity Commission (EEOC).

If you believe that your workplace rights have been violated, your first step should be to discuss the issue with your employer to see if it can be resolved. Check your employee handbook to see what procedures are in place to assist you. If you are not sure, contact your human resources department.

Title VII, the ADA, ADEA, PDA, GINA and the Equal Pay Act (EPA) not only prohibit discrimination in the workplace, but they also allow employees to recover damages against employers who violate these laws. Damages can include loss of pay and benefits as well as compensatory damages for the emotional distress caused by the employer's actions. You may also be able to recover any attorney's fees.

The United States **"Equal Employment Opportunity Commission (EEOC)"** was established to oversee violations of federal laws relating to discrimination in the workplace. For violations of federal discrimination laws, a complaint must be filed with the EEOC before an action in court. However, for violation of the EPA (which prohibits sex discrimination in wages), you may elect to go straight to court.

Filing a Complaint with the EEOC

The EEOC has procedures in place for employees to file a complaint against their employer based on violations of federal laws which prohibit discrimination. A complaint must be filed within 180 or 300 days of the date the discrimination occurred. You get 300 days if a state or local agency enforces a law that prohibits employment discrimination for the same reasons.

Except for violations of the Equal Pay Act, you may not sue your employer in court until you have filed a Charge of Discrimination with the EEOC and have allowed the EEOC to investigate your claims of discrimination. The EEOC has offices throughout the United States. http://www1.eeoc.gov

Filing a Timely EEOC Complaint

You must file within 180 or 300 days from the date the discrimination took place.

- If more than one act occurred, you must file a timely complaint for each act.

- If the harassment or discrimination is ongoing, you must file within 180 or 300 days of the date of the last harassment, even if the earlier acts occurred outside this limit.

You do not need a lawyer to contact the EEOC or to file a Charge of Discrimination.

An EEOC Investigation

Once a complaint is filed per the EEOC rules, the local office will:

1. Determine whether it has jurisdiction over the actions you are complaining about.

2. Investigate complaints of discrimination.

3. Determine if your claim is actionable.

4. Provide alternative assistance for claims that are not actionable.

During the investigation stage, the EEOC may ask you and your employer if you are interested in meeting with an impartial mediator to work out your issues. Mediation is completely voluntary and both sides must agree to it. If you engage in mediation but do not resolve your issues, the EEOC will continue with its investigation and make its recommendations.

If you file a claim with the EEOC, at the conclusion of its investigation, the EEOC may issue you a "Right to Sue" letter that now allows you to file suit against your employer.

REAL LIFE EXAMPLE

This is a sample Title VII Discrimination Complaint.

Gemma Chan has worked at TechCo for ten years as a software designer. During that time, she has successfully developed and implemented many high-profile products. She has always received excellent performance reviews. Her coworker, Greg, has been with TechCo for five years and has worked on lower-profile projects. His manager has rated him as "meeting expectations" all five years.

After a company-wide reorganization, Gemma and Greg are now supervised by Leo. Leo is new to the division and brings two software designers from his old division, Ben and Tyler. Leo, Ben, Tyler and Greg spend a lot of time talking about sports and they often play golf together. The men don't invite Gemma to join them for lunch or to play golf.

Gemma notices that Leo is assigning Ben, Tyler and Greg to work on new high-profile projects while she is stuck on what she feels is "busy work." She also believes that Leo is intentionally excluding her from team-building activities. She files a complaint with TechCo's HR department that Leo is discriminating against her because she is a woman, because of her national origin, which is Chinese and because of her race, Asian.

HR investigates Gemma's claims, speaking to Leo, Ben, Tyler and Greg, but concludes that Leo did not discriminate against her. Two weeks later, Gemma receives her performance review and learns that Leo rated her as "partially meets expectations." Gemma overhears Greg bragging to Tyler that Leo just gave him the best annual review he has ever gotten and that Leo was planning to "stick it" to Gemma.

The following week Leo reassigns Gemma to another low-level project and gives her high-profile project to Ben. Ben shows Gemma an email Leo sent to him that reads, "The Asian chick is going to get what's coming to her after this HR business. Besides, she's had enough opportunities and this will be your chance to really shine."

Gemma goes to the EEOC and files a Charge of Discrimination claiming that she has been discriminated against on the bases of her gender, race and national origin. She also claims that Leo has retaliated against her for going to the HR office with her original claim for discrimination. The EEOC investigates Gemma's claims, including interviewing TechCo management and Leo, Ben, Tyler and Greg. The EEOC issues Gemma a "Right to Sue" letter, and she files a lawsuit.

Different Rules for Federal Government Employees

If you work for the federal government, you must go through an internal administrative process to have your discrimination claims resolved. An administrative judge from the EEOC will determine the merits of your case in a proceeding similar to a lawsuit filed in court.

To learn more about filing an EEOC claim and whether your grievance is covered, check out: http://www.eeoc.gov

Does It Make Sense to Sue My Employer If My Rights Are Violated?

When it comes to suing an employer, there are many factors to consider. Your likelihood of success and what you can recover may be the most practical considerations.

If you believe that your workplace rights have been violated, you have the right to seek a remedy in court. Where and when you file your action depends on the statutes violated.

What Evidence Must I Show?

To win your case, you must prove your case "by a preponderance of the evidence." This means that the judge or jury must believe that what you say is more likely true than not. If the judge or jury is not sure if what you claim is true, then you will lose.

Often winning and losing depends on what you can prove and that's where the nature of evidence becomes very important.

"Direct Evidence" proves a fact without any other information. Circumstantial evidence *tends* to prove a fact. Circumstantial evidence can be just as valuable as direct evidence, so don't be afraid to pursue your claim because you do not have direct evidence of discrimination.

Going back to Gemma's Title VII case, here's how the evidence stacks up:

- Leo's email to Ben is *direct evidence* that Leo was retaliating against her for going to HR about his actions.

- The performance evaluation that Leo gave Gemma rating her as "partially meeting expectations" after he learned that she reported him to the HR office would be *circumstantial evidence* that he was retaliating against her.

- There is *circumstantial evidence* that Leo was discriminating against Gemma because of her gender because she is not invited to lunch with her male coworkers and because Leo has assigned her "busy work" while giving the good assignments to the men.

- Leo's email to Ben also includes circumstantial evidence that tends to prove that Leo is making his employment decisions based on Gemma's gender, race and national origin.

The reality is that few, if any, people are going to make self-incriminating statements that clearly prove a point, so often you must be prepared to submit circumstantial evidence to prove that your employer's actions were more likely than not motivated by illegal discrimination.

What Are My Chances of Winning a Lawsuit?

Ask any lawyer what they think your chances are of winning your lawsuit and you will probably get the answer: "It depends." While the laws should be applied uniformly, every case is "fact specific" and the facts of your situation will determine the outcome of your case.

Other examples of direct evidence might be:

- "We never hire women to operate heavy machinery." (gender discrimination)

- "I don't like Canadians and won't have them on my staff." (national origin discrimination)

- A company hiring memorandum states: "TrendyCo looks for cool, young and hip kids to sell our clothes." (age discrimination)

Examples of circumstantial evidence of illegal discrimination could include:

- Diamond's Department Store only hires young women to work at the cosmetics counter. (age and gender discrimination)

- TechCo gives Roger bad assignments after he files a complaint of disability discrimination. (retaliation)

- Ace Hotel has a history of promoting Caucasian males to management positions from the front desk staff but not women. (gender and race discrimination)

What Money Damages Can I Collect If I Win?

This is another question that lawyers will answer with, "It depends." A judge or jury may award you compensatory damages like back pay for lost wages, and potentially also damages to reimburse you for expenses you incurred for medical or behavioral health care due to the emotional distress you have suffered as a result of discrimination. A court may also award you monetary damages for your pain, suffering and/or emotional distress.

If your case involves age discrimination, the law does not permit an award of damages for emotional distress.

Limits on Awards for Emotional Distress

There is a cap on the total compensatory and punitive damages that can be awarded, depending on the size of the employer.

- For employers with 15-100 employees, the limit is $50,000.

- For employers with 101-200 employees, the limit is $100,000.

- For employers with 201-500 employees, the limit is $200,000.

- For employers with more than 500 employees, the limit is $300,000.

Should I Get a Lawyer?

Often the big issue up front is what it costs to hire a lawyer to represent you. The idea of suing your employer or getting involved in the legal system can be overwhelming and frightening. An attorney who is experienced in your issues will explain your rights and remedies to you and guide you through the process. Emotions often run high in employment cases, and your attorney will be the person who deals directly with your employer (or its attorney) so that you don't have to. While you can represent yourself, a lawyer experienced in your type of case may be the better way to go.

Generally attorney's fees can be awarded if you win your lawsuit in many types of discrimination cases. However, attorney's fees are not awarded under the Age Discrimination in Employment Act and they are not awarded if you lose. As a practical matter, you must be prepared to pay your attorney whether you win or lose your case. Your agreement with your attorney may be based on an hourly charge for legal services, a flat fee, or on a contingency basis (meaning that you will pay your attorney a percentage of whatever amounts you win).

In addition to paying attorney's fees, you may have to pay filing fees and other costs that arise during litigation. These include the cost for depositions (where the parties take testimony out-of-court prior to a trial), copying, postage and other out-of-pocket expenses.

Lawyer Referral

Many state bar associations offer a lawyer referral service. For a small fee, you will be referred to an attorney who specializes in employment law for a one-time consultation. The attorney will give you an assessment of your case, and you and the attorney may agree for the attorney to represent you. You are also free to hire another attorney. Neither you nor the attorney has any obligation to one another after the consultation, although the lawyer is required to keep your consultation confidential.

Thoughts About Suing Your Employer

For many people, filing a lawsuit against their employer is often about more than just money; it's about being proactive to protect their rights and end illegal behavior. The reality of all litigation is that no matter how strongly you and/or your lawyer may feel about your case, you may ultimately lose in court. Sometimes practical reality intervenes and it's important to consider settling!

Particularly if your employer takes a "no holds barred" approach, there may be no way to win, despite a "winning" case. If the employer has significant resources, they will resort to countless "legal" ways to wear you down from delay after delay, to pushing you into accepting a low settlement so you drop your case. Just as you may want to strongly protect rights and end illegal behavior, your employer may have a vested interest in making sure the status quo is not affected—if for no other reason than to deter other employees from following suit.

Consider Settling a Lawsuit

Being involved in a lawsuit can be all-encompassing. You think about it constantly so that both your personal and professional lives suffer. You must spend time responding to requests for information, giving a deposition or sitting in on a deposition of another witness. You may have to sit through a trial and hear people lie about you or your work performance. You are paying attorney's fees. And you may not win.

Once you have raised your employment issues, there are always opportunities for you to settle your dispute. The EEOC often suggests that you mediate with your employer and judges sometimes require parties to engage in settlement negotiations or mediation. Sometimes an employer will not settle and you will have no choice. But if you do, it is often the best way to go.

Advantages of Settling an Employment Case

- By settling, you put an end to the litigation on terms that are acceptable to you.

- A settlement may give you the opportunity to get a result that a court cannot give you. A court can give money damages but it cannot, for example, require an employer to discipline an employee or request an apology from a wrongdoer. In a settlement, you may have more leeway to get this type of result.

- You can get back to your life instead of being consumed by an ongoing lawsuit.

Your Rights on Termination of Employment

When it comes to employment termination, your rights may be governed by state and federal employment laws, any employment agreements you signed, and even your employee handbook (whether or not you ever read it).

At some point you will leave your current employment, whether you are fired, resign or retire. If you have not signed an employment contract, your company may have an employee handbook or employee policies that lay out what happens and what rights and obligations are created when the employment terminates.

Often when employees are hired, they are asked to sign a form that says they have received and read the employee handbook. You may have bound yourself to the termination provisions whether you focused on them or not.

Whatever your reason for leaving, you have certain rights by law in addition to any rights you may have based on the type of "employment relationship."

Employee at Will

Most employers and employees engage in an "at will" employment relationship. This means that your employer may end your employment at any time for any *legal* reason. It also means that *you* may end the employment relationship at any time.

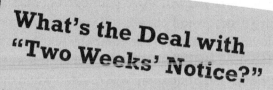

What's the Deal with "Two Weeks' Notice?"

If two weeks' notice is not required by state law, a union agreement or an employment agreement:

- You do not have to give two weeks' notice—or any notice—that you are leaving your job. It may be a good idea to not burn bridges, but may not be legally required.

- Your employer does not have to give you two weeks' notice—or any notice —that your employment is being terminated.

- You are not entitled to severance pay, unless mandated by company policy, employee handbook or a provision of an employment contract

---

Most employers will make it clear either in your engagement letter or the employee handbook that your employment is "at will." This means you can quit or be fired at any time for any legal reason.

Employment Contracts

Some employees have a contract with their employer that goes beyond an engagement letter or job offer that sets forth a job description and rate of pay. High-level executives often have contracts with their employer setting forth very specific terms and conditions of employment as well as termination clauses. These agreements will govern the rules of the road while you are working for the employer and also provide for what happens when your employment is terminated.

If you are planning to quit, check your employment contract or employee handbook to see what is required.

Independent Contractors

In today's world, many employers hire people to work for them who they call **"independent contractors."** In fact, the tax rules very specifically define who is an employee and who is an "independent contractor." And just because an employer calls you a contractor, you may not actually be one under the law.

But assuming you are legally an independent contractor, whether you have signed an agreement to that effect or not, you do not have the same rights that an employee might have. Typically the biggest distinction for a contractor vs. an employee is that contractors do not receive benefits, payment of employment (FICA) taxes, vacation or severance. Accordingly, upon termination, independent contractors have no rights to receive anything but payment for services rendered to date.

Hayley and Michaela are "at will" employees who work in the home goods section at Ruby's Department Store. They learn that Ruby's is considering closing the home goods department in all their stores.

Hayley takes a new job and tells her supervisor at the end of her shift that she is quitting and won't be back. As an "at will" employee, Hayley has no legal obligation to give Ruby's any notice that she is leaving.

A few days later, Ruby's tells Michaela that her employment will be terminated in one month. Ruby's did not have any legal obligation to give Michaela any notice that her job was being terminated but did so as a courtesy to Michaela.

What Do You Get When Terminated?

First and foremost, whether you leave your job voluntarily or are fired, you are entitled to be paid for the time you worked.

- Hourly employees must be paid for all hours worked up until the time of termination, including overtime pay, (but only if you worked in excess of forty hours in the workweek.)

- If you are an exempt employee (e.g., you are paid a weekly salary) and you do not complete a workweek, then your employer may reduce your final pay to reflect time you actually worked.

- You may be entitled to overtime, benefits or other wages depending on what the employer policies, a union agreement or an employment contract provides.

Your right to be paid for accrued vacation and sick leave depends on your state laws as well as your employer's policies.

REAL LIFE EXAMPLES

Sam is a front desk clerk at Ace Hotel. He is an "at will" employee. His workweek runs Monday through Sunday. He works ten hours on Monday, Tuesday and Thursday and quits at the end of the day on Thursday. Sam must be paid for thirty hours at his regular rate of pay. He is not entitled to "overtime" pay just because he worked in excess of eight hours on the days he worked.

Gus is the general manager at Ace Hotel and is a salaried employee. He is paid $2,000 a week. His workweek is also Monday through Sunday. Gus is fired on Wednesday. Ace must pay him for the three days he worked but does not have to pay him his full weekly salary.

When Do You Get Paid After Termination?

Some states require that your employer pay you immediately upon termination of your employment. Absent a specific state requirement, you should be paid for all hours worked at the same time that you would normally receive your wages for that workweek.

Benefits After Termination

Health Insurance. The **"Consolidated Omnibus Budget Reconciliation Act (COBRA)"** provides that certain employees and/or their families may continue their health insurance after termination of employment. Your employer is required to provide you with information regarding your COBRA rights. Even if your employer subsidized the cost of health insurance for employees, once terminated you will be required to pay for the *full cost (plus an administration fee)* to continue your insurance.

If you are receiving severance pay from your employer, it may deduct the cost of COBRA coverage from your severance pay. If there is no pay being received, you will have to pay for the insurance from your own funds. This may create a cash-flow issue.

Unemployment Benefits. You may be entitled to receive unemployment compensation after termination. Unemployment insurance is a joint federal program that provides cash benefits to terminated employees. Each state has its own program which complies with federal guidelines. The amount of benefit is a percentage of your compensation, based on your state's program. Generally, unemployment benefits are not available if you:

- Resign voluntarily.

- Are terminated for cause.

- Have not worked at the employer (or a prior employer) for a period of time required under law.

You can learn about your state's benefits by checking your state's Department of Labor or similar agency.

Pension and Retirement Benefits. The **"Employee Retirement Income Security Act of 1974 (ERISA),"** establishes standards and requirements for employers who create retirement and pension plans for their employees. Your right to these benefits upon termination of your employment is covered by ERISA and other related laws. You can check out http://www.reallifelegal. com for the availability of a guidebook to help you decipher these rules.

You Can't Take It with You

You can't take company property when you leave. This includes:

- Business equipment, e.g., laptops, cell phones and calculators.

- Business supplies, e.g., paper, folders and staplers.

- Customer lists.

- Proprietary information and trade secrets.

Unauthorized removal of company property and, in particular, customer lists and trade secrets, can subject you to both criminal and civil penalties.

Wrapping up Your Departure

Leaving a job can be a stressful time when many things seem may seem unclear about your rights as you leave and the uncertain future ahead. Do your best to nail things down.

What About References?

Having a good reference from your employer may mean the difference between snagging a new job and being unemployed. And references can be a very touchy subject all the way around—for employers and employees both.

Many employers have become wary of providing references—good or bad—for fear of being sued by their employees or their former employee's new employers. As a result, most companies will only verify your job title, dates of employment and your beginning and ending wages.

Valued employees who leave on bad terms, or move on to better opportunities, are often concerned that an employer will intentionally give a bad reference. Many states have enacted laws that protect both employers and employees, allowing employers to provide information on employees as long as it is done in "good faith." Depending on the state, your former employer can tell your prospective employer why you were discharged, the results of any drug or alcohol testing, whether you are eligible for rehire and whether you were subject to any disciplinary action.

If this is a concern for you, make sure you check your state's Department of Labor or similar agency to learn the laws in your state. *Former employers may not be reliable for a good reference, but an individual at your former place of employment may be. Make sure you know the lay of the land before you give out references.*

Termination/Severance Agreements

In today's workplace, employers can be aggressive in asking employees to sign away rights and other opportunities in a severance agreement. Often employees, facing the stress of being fired or laid off, accept what's offered, fearing that if they negotiate they may lose their right to severance payments or unemployment. There is a lot of confusion and fear in these situations because employees are vulnerable and it often seems that employers hold the power.

Don't assume that everything presented to you is fair or legal or proper. Often there is room to negotiate.

Common Terms in Severance Agreements

- Severance pay.
- Benefit continuation for a period of time.
- Use of company resources.
- Out-placement services.
- Promise of good references absent termination for cause.
- Retention of company property such as a car, computer or cell phone.

If you are being terminated or laid off as part of a group of people being laid off, or you are a valued employee who may have some leverage to negotiate a better deal for yourself, make sure you give it a go before merely accepting what an employer offers. In a group layoff involving a union contract, special rules apply and they are not covered here.

If you are terminated, you are absolutely entitled to wages for services performed, unreimbursed expenses that were legitimately incurred, and COBRA continuation medical coverage if you were covered by a company health plan. An agreement offered which does not include them is not a proper offer.

If you are age forty or over, any termination agreement you receive will ask you to waive your rights under the ADEA and the appropriate waiver language must be in the agreement. If the proper language is not there, it's important to make sure you know your rights and consult with an attorney about the consequences.

Hire a Lawyer to Review Your Severance/ Termination Agreement

Many people are afraid to hire a lawyer to review a termination agreement because they:

- Are ashamed or embarrassed that they have been terminated.

- Fear looking foolish for not understanding the agreement, the law or their rights.

- Don't know an attorney or are afraid of what it will cost.

If you don't understand the agreement being offered, or have any questions about whether it is fair or legal, we recommend you hire an attorney to review it. Emotions like anger and fear may run high and an attorney may be the best way to protect your rights and make sure you are getting a fair deal. At the least, consulting an attorney can give you peace of mind that you've done what you can. A brief consultation with an attorney through a lawyer referral service may be all you need to set your mind at ease.

Nothing Ventured, Nothing Gained

In all sorts of legal dealings, the party handing over the agreement designs it to be intimidating—often with the hope that the person who receives it will feel they have no choice but to sign. But you may have a choice. Don't be afraid to inquire about terms or negotiate a severance agreement.

REAL LIFE EXAMPLE

Cameron was an executive employed by Magic Advertising for fifteen years. The employee handbook provided that each employee would get two weeks' severance for every year worked at Magic, if they were terminated without cause. Magic announced it was closing Cameron's division, and she was offered a severance package that:

- Permitted her to have access to the office for three months.

- Let her keep her company computer.

- Gave her some payment towards COBRA coverage.

- Included thirty weeks of severance (two weeks for each year of work).

The offer seemed quite generous but the fine print stated that Cameron: (1) could not work *at all* while collecting her severance; (2) had to repay all severance if she went to work for another advertising agency within a year of termination and (3) had to turn over tax returns, and pay stubs, to verify that she did not work during this period.

Cameron had worked in advertising for her whole career and was eager to get another job in advertising, but didn't want to forfeit the severance or lose her right to COBRA coverage. Cameron knew her colleagues had signed the agreements with the objectionable language because they were afraid to "make waves" or "lose their right to health insurance."

Cameron consulted an attorney who advised that she could not legally lose her right to health insurance. He also reviewed the Magic Advertising Employee Handbook and discovered that the severance was not conditioned on Cameron's promise not to work or not to work for another advertising agency. The attorney felt strongly that this would not be legally enforceable.

Cameron told Magic she had consulted an attorney and that he had recommended she not sign the agreement. At first Magic responded that all other terminated employees had signed as is. Cameron stood firm and was able to negotiate the language out. By hiring an attorney to help her, Cameron preserved her right to continue to work and collect severance. It was worth the attorney's fee.

Closing Thoughts

14

Labor laws and workplace rights are an ever-changing area of the law. Laws to prevent discrimination are increasingly being passed on a state and local level. Be sure to check out your state's Department of Labor and city laws if you believe you are subject to illegal discrimination or termination.

An attorney may be your best ally if you find yourself in a tough situation at work, with an employer or negotiating a severance agreement. If you have a particular situation not addressed here, check out the plentiful resources online at government websites (http://www.eeoc.gov and http://www.dol.gov) to get help. They offer a lot of information and may give you a jump-start on your specific concerns.

Some matters affecting employment are regulated at both the state and federal level. States also have web sites that can help workers learn their rights protected at the state level. States often have their own labor laws and laws regulating workplace safety and workplace hours. So make sure to check out information from your state's Department of Labor if you have an issue and need help.

If you don't have the resources to hire an attorney, check out local bar associations and legal aid societies in your area because they often can point you in the right direction for free or low-cost services

Glossary

ADEA Waiver: Document which employers ask employees to sign upon termination that provides that the employee "waives" the right to sue the employer based on age discrimination. Federal law, under the Age Discrimination in Employment Act, spells out what this waiver must provide to be legally enforceable.

Age Discrimination in Employment Act (ADEA): Federal law which makes it illegal to discriminate against employees who are age forty and older and applies to employers with twenty or more employees.

Americans with Disabilities Act (ADA): Federal law that prohibits discrimination on the basis of a person's disability.

"At Will" Employment: This means your employer can fire you at any time without notice and you may quit at any time without notice.

Bona Fide Occupational Qualification (BFOQ): Relates to whether an aspect of a job is essential for purposes of determining whether a person meets job requirements. An employer would have a BFOQ if it required female models for a fashion show of women's clothes.

Business Necessity: Relates to whether an employer's policy for a particular job description or requirement is needed because of the business. Skyscraper window washers not being afraid of heights is an example of business necessity.

Circumstantial Evidence: Proof that tends to establish a fact, often when pieced together with other evidence.

Civil Rights Act of 1964: Federal law which made it illegal to discriminate on the basis of race, color, religion, national origin or gender.

COBRA (Consolidated Omnibus Budget Reconciliation Act): Mandates that employees and their families be provided with continued health coverage after termination of employment, or upon the happening of other events (e.g., divorce). The employee must pay for this coverage at his or her own expense.

Code of Federal Regulations (CFR): Administrative rules to implement federal laws.

Constructive Discharge: When a person is forced to quit a job because an employer's illegal conduct has forced him or her to leave.

Direct Evidence: Proves a fact, without any other information. For example, a file of attendance records shows the employer kept attendance records.

Discrimination: In the employment context, discrimination occurs when a person who is in a "protected" class is treated less favorably than others upon hiring, during employment or upon termination.

Disparate Impact: Term to describe an employment policy that looks fair and neutral but is not. It is a legal term used to describe whether illegal discrimination is present.

Disparate Treatment: Treating similarly situated employees differently. Legal term used to assess whether illegal discrimination is present.

Employee Retirement Income Security Act of 1974 (ERISA): Establishes standards and requirements for employers who provide pensions/retirement benefits for employees.

Glossary

Equal Employment Opportunity Commission (EEOC): Federal agency that oversees federal laws related to workplace discrimination and has a complaint-and-hearing process for discrimination claims.

Equal Pay Act (EPA): Federal law that requires employers to pay men and women at the same rate for equal work.

Essential Job Function: Under the Americans with Disabilities Act, even a person with a disability must still be able to do the job, with or without a disability. If the job is to be a seamstress, the ability to sew is an essential job function.

Genetic Information Act of 2008: Federal law that prohibits an employer from using or obtaining genetic information about a person or the person's family in order to make employment decisions.

Hostile Workplace Environment: Work environment where harassment or discrimination is so severe or pervasive that a reasonable person would consider it abusive, hostile or intimidating.

Independent Contractor: This is a term of art which refers to a person who is not an employee and works as an outside hire for an employer. Independent contractors (under the tax definition) pay their own social security (employment taxes), benefits and tax withholding. They typically receive no employee benefits such as paid vacation or worker's compensation.

Major Life Activities: Under the Americans With Disabilities Act, a person is deemed to have a disability if there is an impairment which "substantially limits" a major life activity. These include things like walking, standing, talking and caring for oneself, as well as major body functions such as kidneys, circulation and breathing.

Pregnancy Discrimination Act (PDA): Prohibits employers from discriminating against women on the basis of their pregnancy.

Protected Class: A group of persons defined by a shared characteristic (e.g., age, national origin, gender) who are frequently discriminated against, and for which federal and/or state laws provide redress.

Reasonable Accommodation: A change that is deemed reasonable for an employer to make to better enable a disabled person to perform a job.

Retaliation: An act that occurs when employment decisions are made against a person because he or she reported discrimination or participated in an investigation concerning discrimination.

Sexual Harassment: A form of "hostile work environment" that makes someone uncomfortable by virtue of their sex, or requires them to engage in behavior which may include sexual favors for a job benefit.

Substantially Limits: Standard under the ADA to determine whether an impairment so affects a major life activity that a person is deemed to have a disability.

Wrongful Termination: An end to employment for reasons that are illegal.

About the Author

Joanne Dekker

Joanne Dekker focuses her practice on employment law, construction and government contract litigation and general business litigation. She is also an avid animal lover and increasingly works on legal issues involving pets and animals. Ms. Dekker represents both management and employees in private sector employment law matters and also represents federal employees before the U.S. Equal Employment Opportunity Commission.

Ms. Dekker graduated *cum laude* from the Catholic University of America in Washington, D.C. with a B.A. in American history. She received the John Farrell Prize for American History and was inducted into Phi Alpha Theta, the international honor society for history. She also earned her J.D. at the Columbus School of Law at Catholic University.

Ms. Dekker is admitted to practice in Maryland, Virginia and the District of Columbia. She is also admitted in the federal courts: United States District Court for the District of Maryland, Eastern District of Virginia and the Court of Appeals for the Federal Circuit. Ms. Dekker is also a member of the Loudoun County Animal Advisory Committee.

About Real Life Legal™

Parker Press Inc., the publisher of Real Life Legal™ creates plain language consumer information on legal, tax, business and financial subjects. Taking aim at info overload and legalese, Parker Press Inc. launched Real Life Legal™ in 2014. Real Life Legal™ provides practical advice, written by lawyers, to help people understand how the law works. Our goal is to provide solid, easy-to-understand information so *you* can decide whether it makes sense to hire a lawyer. Real Life Legal™ wants you to be prepared.

Available Titles

Bankruptcy Basics: Chapter 7 and Chapter 13
Marina Ricci, Esq.

Business Owners Startup Guide
Susan G. Parker, Esq. and Lynne Williams, Esq.

Elder Law: Legal Planning for Seniors
Susan G. Parker, Esq. and Maria B. Whealan, Esq.

Employee's Guide to Discrimination and Termination
Joanne Dekker, Esq.

Estate Planning: A Road Map for Beginners
Susan G. Parker, Esq. and Maria B. Whealan, Esq.

Filing a Homeowner's Claim: Natural Disaster or Not
Dawn Snyder, Esq.

A Lawyer's Guide to Home Renovations
John A. Goodman, Esq.

Available Titles (Continued)

Planning for Pets: Trusts, Leash Laws and More
Joanne Dekker, Esq.

Planning for Your Special Needs Child
Amy Newman, Esq.

Special Needs Education: Navigating for Your Child
Lynne Williams, Esq.

U.S. Veterans: Your Rights and Benefits
Maria B. Whealan, Esq.
with Paul M. Goodson, Esq.

What to Do When Someone Dies
Susan G. Parker, Esq.

You've Been Arrested: Now What?
Maryam Jahedi, Esq.

Notes

Notes

Notes

Notes

Notes

Notes

Notes

Notes

Notes

Notes

Notes